TURKISH COOKERY

BY

NEZIH SIMON

KU-110-152

ILLUSTRATED BY

JEAN PAPWORTH

Tredolphin Press

Nezih Simon's explanations are disarmingly simple and clear — her recipes work for experts and novices alike — and are based on a life time of experience. The author originated the first cookery and domestic science classes in Cyprus, and at the age of seventeen she unexpectedly found herself acting headmistress with the task of starting the first Turkish girl's boarding school on the island. On her return to England, she helped to pioneer the teaching of cooking to partially sighted children; formerly it had been considered too risky.

'shish your own Kebab'

CONTENTS

Author's Preface

My mother hated amateurs in the kitchen! She cooked so well herself; and if she was not there we had a cook. So I did not even have to boil the customary egg!

I was persuaded to take up cookery training because of local needs. Domestic Science was going to be taught at secondary schools in Cyprus and they needed trained teachers. I was one of the few people sent to England to get that training. As soon as I started the training I loved it and have enjoyed cooking ever since, whether teaching or cooking at home; I ought to add here that strange as it may seem, recipe books aren't used in Cyprus or Turkey, so one has to learn by practice.

My family and friends have all encouraged me in my efforts to produce Turkish dishes. Naturally, knowing a lot of ways of cooking adds variety to our everyday cooking and therefore lessens the monotony attached to routine.

My daughter often comes into the kitchen for little chats and it was she who asked me to write down my recipes. She said, 'it will be my most treasured gift'; I could not ignore such a request or refuse and so 'Shish your own Kebab' materialised.

My most sincere thanks to all members of my family and friends who sampled the dishes or helped in numerous other ways, especially my brother-in-law Simon Grove, who has done so much to get this book off the ground.

I must also acknowledge the efforts of my friend Jean Papworth, who drew the illustrations; Jill Vasey, who designed the art-work and layout; and Juliet Crombie, who edited the drafts.

Keats Grove   Nezih Simon
Hampstead
1968

Introduction

The Ottoman Empire, Mozart, military bands, cooking, the British Household Cavalry — what more incongruous collection could one find? Yet they all have a common link with the corps of Jannissaries of Imperial Turkey. This was a corps d'élite, a Pretorian Guard, whose military skill and measured step into battle cast fear into the hearts of opposing armies and dominated the battlefields of Eastern Europe and the Middle East for hundreds of years.

They originated in a nucleus of Christian slaves forcibly converted to Islam; their ranks were replenished by a compulsory levy on Christian children, who were taken at an early age, trained, disciplined and indoctrinated so as to become a magnificent fighting machine for the Ottoman Emperors. The slaves from whom they were originally recruited must have been employed in the kitchens, for many of the military ranks still recalled gastronomy. And when they went into battle their cooking pots were carried on a cart and formed a rallying point in war. So that they could be located easily during a battle, the Turks stretched skins over the top of the brass cauldrons and beat them with ladles, thus originating the kettle drum. Other countries started to copy their military methods and their military band, so that Mozart wrote Turkish marches and the mounted band of the Household Cavalry is led by a drumhorse with kettle drums hanging on either side of the saddle. Even the plumed helmets of the Household Cavalry may owe their origin to the horse tails which designated ranks in the Ottoman Army. And so, as the military might of the Ottoman Empire spread far and wide, traditions of Turkish cookery followed in its wake.

The Ottoman Turks loved to eat well and as their riches and splendour increased, so did the extravagance of their cooking. The banquets started with a variety of scented waters for washing hands and ended in sipping Turkish coffee and drinking sherbet. Many people have written about these banquets: the splendour of their china and gold plates; the gorgeous costumes of those who waited at table. It has all become a legend. The Ottoman Turks dominated most of the Middle East, so that these countries could not help but be influenced in their cooking habits. Some national dishes (mainly Persian and Assyrian) which the Sultans liked were absorbed into the everyday life of the Palace. After the fall of the Empire, the Turks kept this love of good food and still do even today. No matter how poor a Turkish home is, you will find at least three or four different dishes at their table. Whether this will survive the modern trend, or rather cult, of keeping slim by nibbling a few lettuce leaves, I do not know. One of the reasons why I felt I ought to write down my favourite recipes was so that my children might be tempted to use them.

At home I often mix English and Turkish cooking. That is why I have chosen recipes which I think mingle well with English dishes and yet add originality to the menu. And most important, I have only given recipes, the ingredients for which can be found in this country.

This book is dedicated to MY MOTHER without whose help nothing would have been possible.

Hors d'oeuvres, Dips and Mezes

In Turkey, Cyprus and all over the Middle East dinners are eaten late. People enjoy sitting and drinking with family and friends, in open-air cafes, by the sea, or on the balcony or verandahs of their houses — waiting for the cool breezes before the serious business of eating starts. The drinks usually served are Ouzo and Brandy Sour, both local drinks.

Turks always take a little food with their drinks. This food is called Meze. Meze is a Turkish word meaning appetizer or hors d'oeuvres. In its simplest form, when found for example in a village cafe, it might be a few slices of tomatoes or a bowl of salted almonds or olives. At its most luxurious, served on the verandah of a three-star hotel, it might almost rival a Scandinavian Smorgesbrod.

In the next few pages, I have chosen practical recipes which can also be used as sauces or dips at cocktail parties.

PATLICAN HUMUSU

(AUBERGINE HUMUS)

(Dip or Sauce)

2 medium-sized aubergines   2—3 hours

2 dessertspoons tahini

Juice of 1 large lemon

½ teaspoon salt

Put aubergines, just as they are, to cook slowly (see above). Leave them for a few hours, turning every so often until they are so well cooked that they turn dark brown and soft. Slit open the skin and scrape the inside into a bowl. Cream it with a fork, add the tahini, lemon juice and salt and continue creaming. More lemon juice can be added if necessary. The mixture should have the consistency of mayonnaise and can be thinned by adding water.

Serve on a dish, decorate the top with finely chopped parsley, a few drops of olive oil, a sprinkle of red pepper and a few pomegranate seeds if available.

2

CACIK
(CUCUMBERS IN YOGURT)

2 cartons plain yogurt   10 minutes

1 cucumber

1 teaspoon dried mint

Salt to taste

Beat the yogurt in a bowl with a little salt until it is runny. You might need to add one teaspoon of water if yogurt is still thick. Into this add previously peeled and very finely chopped cucumber and the mint. Keep in the fridge and serve cold.

It can also be served as the first course at a dinner party. This is the same beverage, without the cucumber, that is sold in the streets of Turkey. in the summer as 'Ayran' which makes a very refreshing drink.

HUMUS (with Chick Peas)
(Dip or Sauce)

1 lb Chick Peas

1 tablespoon salt

½ lb Tahini (Sesame oil)

Juice of 3 or 4 lemons

Parsley

Red Pepper

Olive oil

1 tablespoon bicarbonate of soda

Soak chick peas overnight in cold water with 1 tablespoon of Bicarbonate of Soda. The following day throw away that water and cook in an ordinary saucepan for two to three hours until the peas are soft. On the other hand if you use a pressure cooker it cuts cooking time to one hour. This is then sieved or put through the mixer, and tahini and lemon juice is added alternately until it reaches the consistency of thick mayonnaise. It can be further thinned by the addition of water. Decorate with chopped parsley, red pepper and olive oil. Serve as a dip with squares of bread or plain with chicken or steak.

DASHI

(TAHINI & LEMON DIP)

¼ pint Tahini   15 minutes

6 liquid ozs.warm water

Juice of one lemon

Garlic salt to taste

Parsley and red pepper

1 tablespoon olive oil

Put tahini into a basin and add warm water gradually, alternating with lemon juice until the mixture is creamy. Put into dishes and decorate the top with finely chopped parsley, red pepper and about one tablespoon of olive oil. Serve with squares of bread.

4

YALANÇI DOLMA

(AUBERGINES: VINE LEAVES FILLED WITH RICE)

4 aubergines	Pressure cooker 10 minutes
4 onions	Ordinary saucepan 30 minutes
1 cup oil	
1 lb rice	
1½ cups water	
1 tablespoon dried mint	
1 teaspoon cinnamon	
1 teaspoon salt	

ALTERNATIVE RECIPE

½ lb vine leaves

Wash aubergines, remove the inside and put it into a saucepan with chopped-up onions and oil. Saute for a few minutes. Add the rice and 1½ cups of water, the mint, cinnamon and salt. When the water is absorbed, remove from the fire and let it cool. Fill the aubergine cases with the stuffing, put them into a pressure cooker, add two cups of water and cook for 10 minutes. Leave to cool. Keep in the refrigerator as they are best eaten when cold.

This recipe can be varied by the addition of vine leaves. Soak the vine leaves in hot water for ½ hour then place each vine leaf on a saucer, using the same rice filling as above. Put approximately 1 dessertspoonful on to the vine leaf, fold the two ends over and roll. Put these neatly at the bottom of the saucepan, add water and place a saucer on top of the vine leaves to keep them in position. Cover and cook slowly for ½ - ¾ hour. These are also best eaten cold.

BULGUR KÖFTE

(WHEAT PASTE FILLED WITH MEAT)

1 lb crushed wheat   1 hour

1 lb minced meat

½ bunch parsley

2 ozs. pine nuts

1 teaspoon cinnamon

¼ lb sultanas

Oil for frying

Wash the crushed wheat and leave it soaking in cold water. Separate half the mince and mix it with finely chopped parsley, salt and cinnamon. Cook this mixture with quarter of a cup of water and 2 tablespoons of oil in a frying pan. Add pine nuts and sultanas and cook for 1 minute more until the water is all absorbed. Leave to cool. Strain the crushed wheat and with the remaining minced meat pass it through the finest mincer. This will now be soft like dough. Make a cone shape with a hole in the centre, fill the hole with the cooked mince, stick the ends by shaping to a point and fry in hot fat until brown. Serve hot or cold.

6

TUZLU PADEM

(SALTED ALMONDS)

½ hour

Take dried kernels of almonds, sprinkle them with very salty water and bake in an oven until nicely brown.

Water melon seeds are also delicious prepared in this way.

OTHER IDEAS FOR COCKTAIL PARTIES

1. Fresh raw vegetables such as pieces of cauliflower or slices of tomatoes, sprinkled with very finely chopped parsley and onions.

2. Slices of cucumber with black olives and a lemon dressing.

3. Crushed fresh green olives with a touch of garlic and coriander seeds.

4. Balls of yogurt with an olive oil dressing. These are made by straining yogurt through a muslin overnight and rolling it into round balls in the palm of the hand.

Ouzo and Brandy Sour are the most popular before-dinner drinks.

Ouzo diluted with water goes milky white and opalescent — in many ways like Pernod and Anisette.

Brandy Sour can be made with French Brandy just as well as with Turkish Brandy, with a slice of fresh lemon and ginger ale added.

A permissible western variant would be Martini; an intriguing newcomer on the English market called Nichol - off Red Vodka, based on an ancient recipe from the south of Russia; or, of course, whisky and soda.

The wine lover can drink any light wines as a chilled, light sherry, white wines or rosé wines, still or sparkling.

Soups

Soups come into their own during the month of Ramazan.
For thirty days during this month every meal is started
with soup, therefore it has to be good to stand this test.
On the other hand, it has to be fairly plain as after the
fasting of the day the first nourishment has to be easily
digested.

As people fast during the day, the nights are usually
gay, with people giving parties where eating is the main
objective. All types of delicacies are prepared and people
enjoy eating while they can. Just before sunrise, they wash
out their mouths, brush their teeth and then everyone is
ready for the long fast.

Ramazan needs tremendous self-control as no food or drink should pass between the lips from sunrise to sunset. Work must go on as usual, even though tempers cannot always stand the strain.

At last the sunset comes and this is the eagerly awaited signal. Coloured lights go on on all the minarets and the muezzin starts the evening prayer.

And now for a few mouthfuls of that soup. In these recipes, I have used pressure cooker continually as it cuts down the cooking time considerably, but if the more conventional saucepan is preferred, directions for this have been given. But I personally would advise a pressure cooker for soups.

The following selection of recipes has been restricted to thick soups as vegetable soups do not vary much from one country to another.

MERCIMEK ÇORBASI

(LENTIL SOUP)

2 ozs. margarine	Pressure cooker 10 minutes
1 medium onion	Ordinary saucepan 30 minutes
2 pints broth	
½ cup lentils	
¼ cup rice	
1 tablespoon salt	
Juice of 1 lemon	

Melt the margarine, add chopped onion, when soft add broth. As soon as it comes to the boil add the lentils, rice salt and the juice of one lemon. This recipe can be varied by the addition of a few sticks of celery, which when cooked ought to be sieved into the lentil mixture and served as cream of lentil soup.

TRAHANA ÇORBASI

(WHEAT SOUP)

5 sticks trahana	Pressure cooker 10 minutes
2 pints broth	Ordinary saucepan 30 minutes
1 tablespoon salt	

Trahana is a mixture of wheat and yogurt cooked together and dried in the hot sun. It is bought in sticks and by the pound. These can be kept in a tin or glass jar just like other cereals.

Soak about 5 sticks of trahana in a little cold water for a few hours. Bring the broth to the boil. Add the soaked trahana and the salt. Before serving add some fried croutons or squares of fried Cyprus cheese called Hellim.

DÜĞÜN ÇORBASI

(WEDDING SOUP)

1 lb mutton or beef	½ hour
1 tablespoon fat	

2 tablespoons flour

1 egg

Juice of 1 lemon

The meat must be lean and cut into one inch cubes. Put these with water and cook until the meat is tender. In another saucepan melt the fat, add the flour and make a white sauce with the liquid in which the meat was cooked. When this sauce has come to the boil, pour it over the pieces of meat and cook over a low heat, stirring occasionally. If too thick, add a little water. Keep to the consistency of a thick soup. Just before serving, beat the egg with the lemon juice and add to the soup. Bring to the boil and serve with a sprinkling of red pepper and some warm melted butter. This soup can be made with chicken instead.

YAYLA ÇORBASI

(COUNTRY SOUP)

¼ lb rice   20 minutes

1 pint water

1 pint yogurt

1 tablespoon chopped mint

2 tablespoons butter

Cook the rice with some salt and water. Beat the yogurt in a bowl, add to the cooked rice and boil together. Melt butter in a frying pan and add to the soup, stir and serve with a sprinkling of mint.

PİRİNÇ ÇORBASI

(RICE SOUP)

2 pints broth   20 minutes

1 cup rice

1 egg or meat balls

Juice of 1 lemon

Salt

2 ozs. margarine

Boil the broth with the rice and salt and when the rice is almost cooked, add beaten egg and stir. Boil for another few minutes. Just before taking off the stove add lemon juice and serve. If egg is not used, add a few meat balls which have been previously prepared, the recipe for which can be found under meat ball soup. Boil the meat balls with the soup, add lemon juice and serve.

KABAK ÇORBASI

(PUMPKIN SOUP)

1 small pumpkin   ½ hour

¼ pint cream

A little milk

Seasoning

Wash, peel and cut up a small pumpkin. Boil in water until soft. Pass it through a sieve, return to the pan and add the cream and a little milk according to the required thickness. Add seasoning, boil it up and serve.

TOPARLAKLI ÇORBA

(MEAT BALL SOUP)

½ lb minced meat   ½ hour

1 coffee cup of rice

½ cup water

salt and pepper

1 egg

Juice of 1 lemon

Mix the minced meat, salt and pepper with rice and water in a bowl. When this is mixed well make small sized meat balls. Half fill a medium sized saucepan with water. When the water is boiling drop the meat balls one by one into the boiling water. When the water in the saucepan is half the original amount, that is to say the meat balls have been cooking for about fifteen minutes, beat an egg in a basin with the lemon juice and a little of the liquor from the meat and add to the rest. Bring to the boil and serve.

ISPANAH ÇORBASI

(SPINACH SOUP)

2 lb spinach   ½ hour

A few meat balls   (see previous recipe)

¼ cup single cream

1 cup of broth

Seasoning

Wash well and cut spinach into 2 inch squares. Cook until soft. Pass it through a sieve and return to the saucepan. Add one cup of bone stock and seasoning. As it comes up to the boil, add ¼ cup of single cream. Stir and add a few meat balls or dumplings, whichever is preferred. (The most usual is meat balls). As spinach is an uneconomical vegetable, it is no use cooking less than 2 lbs of it.

Vegetables

In the Middle East, vegetables are plentiful, in spite of irrigation problems, or because of them; people have to work twice as hard to grow several different crops through the year. Even children are bribed into carrying buckets of water in the early morning to revive parched marrows, water melon or rows of cucumbers or tomatoes, as practically everyone in Cyprus has a little vegetable garden and freshness of vegetables seems to be the key to everything. Still, they are lucky to have the best of both worlds, as they have European and Asian vegetables of such variety and abundance that this naturally leads to a rich cuisine. Another factor is the lack of lush grazing lands. People are therefore dependent on lamb or mutton for meat, and goats for milk and cheese. It is not therefore surprising that they have a whole series of recipes using meat and vegetables cooked slowly together. This method we call 'Basti' or stew. The joy of this type of cooking is that it can be cooked the previous day if necessary, as it improves when re-heated.

At dinner parties these 'basti' add originality as side dishes, and are more nourishing for growing children than plain vegetables. We also have a whole set of recipes for cooking vegetables with meat fillings. These recipes are simple to prepare, too, and add just a touch of the exotic, yet blend well with the English taste — and, what is more, are within the means of most of us.

Perhaps a better known method in Europe is 'Moussaka' where each item of meat and vegetable is first sautéd, then put into a casserole and cooked slowly.

My favourites are cooked vegetables served cold as salads, and of course, raw vegetables served in the same way: tomatoes with such fine skins that they melt in the mouth, or Kohlrabi, so crisp that it holds a salad together.

In the following pages I have only given recipes which would appeal to the European taste; I have left out some spices which are not great favourites with my family. I have also left out garlic, but if desired, a little garlic can be added to all the recipes.

PATLICAN DOLMASI

(STUFFED AUBERGINES)

3 aubergines   45 minutes

1 cup corn oil

1 onion

½ lb minced meat

Parsley

2 fresh tomatoes

1 tablespoon tomato sauce

This quantity is sufficient for two people.

Partly peel aubergines in strips and make a slit in the centre of each, large enough to be able to remove the inside. Roll the aubergines in slightly salted hot fat for a second on each side. Remove them from the pan and let them cool. Cook chopped onion in the same fat for about 2 minutes. Add minced meat, finely chopped parsley, salt and pepper according to taste, and about ½ cup of water. Cook until all the fat and water is absorbed. Then fill the aubergines with this mixture. Put in a casserole or baking dish, with a slice of tomato on top of each slit. Now mix the tomato sauce with a cup of water and add to the aubergines in the casserole. Cook in a medium oven for about 45 minutes or in a saucepan, with just enough water to cover the aubergines, and a saucer on top to keep them down, until tender.

KABAK DOLMASI

(STUFFED COURGETTES)

50 minutes

4 courgettes   Parsley

½ lb minced meat   1 fresh tomato

1 onion   2 tablespoons oil

Peel the courgettes in strips. Cut one end and remove the inside. Roll them in hot fat, let them cool and fill with the same mixture as for the stuffed aubergines. Place the filled courgettes at the bottom of a saucepan. Add two tablespoonfuls of oil and water to cover. Season with salt and pepper, put a saucer on top of the vegetables, cover with a lid and cook gently.

Another way of cooking Stuffed Courgettes is to leave all the ingredients raw, but add a ¼ cup of rice to the mince. Leave the courgettes clean but raw, and stuff them. Cook the same way.

SOĞAN DOLMASI

(STUFFED ONIONS)

1 large onion   ½ hour

Same stuffing as above

The flavour of these blends very well with that of courgettes, so you can add one or two while cooking courgettes.

Take one large onion, top and tail it and split down one side. Leave in hot water. After a few minutes it will peel layer by layer. Take one layer and using the same stuffing, fill it, and putting the split side downwards, place it between the courgettes and cook in the same manner.

İNGİNAR DOLMASI

(STUFFED ARTICHOKES)

20 minutes

4 artichokes   1 onion

½ lb minced meat   Parsley

Gently remove the beards from the centres of the artichokes. Remove the tough leaves on the outside. Fill the centres with the same minced meat stuffing as for previous recipes and cook gently for about 20 minutes in the same way.

BİBER DOLMASI

(STUFFED GREEN PEPPERS)

¾ hour

The same process is used, and the same stuffing. In fact, mixed vegetables go rather well together. You could use 3 aubergines and 3 green peppers and cook them together.

With all these vegetables it is advisable to serve a plain rice pilaff, or a crushed wheat pilaff. Every Turkish dinner table contains a pilaff of some sort, or a salad. You could not wish for a better balanced meal.

PİRİNÇ PİLAVI

(PLAIN RICE PILAFF)

1 cup rice   ½ hour

1½ cups broth

½ teaspoon salt

2 oz margarine or butter

At least half an hour before you intend cooking the rice, blanche it (i.e., pour boiling water over it and leave it to stand). Drain the rice before use.

Pour the broth into a saucepan, and when it starts to boil, pour the rice in and add the salt. Reduce the heat and let it simmer until all moisture is absorbed and little holes show on the surface. Then switch off the heat, cover with a towel and leave for 5 to 10 minutes. Warm the butter and pour over it. Stir and serve. If, however, you have used rich chicken broth there is no need for extra butter.

For a rich pilaff, see page 46.

BULGUR PİLAVI

(CRUSHED WHEAT PILAFF)

1½ cups broth   ½ hour

1 cup crushed wheat (Bulgur)

½ teaspoon salt

2 oz butter

Pour the broth into a saucepan and when it starts to boil, add the wheat. Lower the heat until all moisture is absorbed and air holes appear on the surface. Switch the heat off. Add butter, stir and allow to stand. Serve in about fifteen minutes.

This pilaff is excellent with braised steak or any of the stuffed vegetables, and makes an interesting change from rice pilaff.

PANCAR YEMEĞİ

(BEETROOT LEAVES OR SHOOTS)

2 lbs fresh beetroots with shoots   60 minutes

½ cup oil

1 onion

½ lb best end of neck

I found to my amazement that most greengrocers in this country chop off the shoots when selling you young beetroots, so for this recipe, ask your greengrocer not to. This dish can only be made when beet are in season.

Chop up the shoots to one inch long. Wash and peel the beetroots, chop into half and slice. Put oil into a saucepan and heat, add chopped onion, meat, also chopped into pieces, and beetroots. Add water just to cover. Add salt and pepper and cook gently for about one hour until vegetables and meat are tender. Serve with a plain yogurt as sauce and a pilaff.

YUVARLAK KÖFTE

(MEAT BALLS)

½ lb minced meat   20 minutes

1 slice stale bread

Parsley

Put minced meat into a basin. Grate one slice of stale bread into this, then add finely chopped parsley and salt. Mix well and shape into round balls in the palm of your hand. Fry in hot fat until brown.

YUVARLAKLI KÖFTE

(SPINACH WITH MEAT BALLS)

	½ hour
2 lbs spinach	½ cup oil
1 onion	Meat Balls
1 tomato	½ cup water
Parsley	

Wash spinach thoroughly and chop as small as you can on a board. Put oil into a saucepan and heat. Add chopped onion, tomato and spinach. Let it all simmer for a while until the spinach produces juice. Now add previously prepared meat balls and the water and cook until tender. Serve with fresh radishes and wheat pilaff.

BAMYA

(LADIES FINGERS)

1 lb ladies fingers (fresh)	½ hour

24

½ lb minced meat or best end of neck

Parsley

Onion

2 tomatoes

¼ cup oil

Wash ladies fingers and remove the tops. Do not cut off the heads otherwise they disintegrate. Heat the oil in a saucepan and add chopped parsley, onion, tomatoes and cooked minced meat or uncooked best end of neck. After a few minutes, cover with water and boil. When boiling add ladies fingers and cook gently until meat and vegetables are tender (about ½ an hour). Serve hot.

All these vegetable dishes can be served as side dishes at parties but they also make a balanced meal on their own, with pilaff and a green salad.

KOLĂKAZ

(STEWED YAM)

1 large head of Yam	1 hour

3 fresh tomatoes or tomato sauce

½ lb of lamb cutlets or pieces of chicken

¼ cup of cooking oil

3 cups of water

This is a root vegetable, and a great favourite with Cypriot Turks, which is a delicacy on the mainland as they do not grow it in Turkey.

Peel the yam like a potato, wash and dry (as it is liable to get sticky). Then crack pieces off the vegetable. Do not wash again. Heat fat in a saucepan and add tomato sauce or chopped fresh tomatoes, stir and add the meat. Stir once or twice, add the pieces of yam and enough water to cover. Now add salt, black pepper and the juice of one lemon and cook gently for one hour. That is until tender.

You see different yams vary in cooking time. Serve with a green salad or raw radishes. If required pieces of chicken can be used instead of cutlets.

TAZE FASULYA

(RUNNER BEANS)

1 lb fresh or frozen beans   ½ hour

¼ cup oil

1 onion

½ lb minced meat or pieces of meat

1 tablespoon tomato sauce or 3 fresh tomatoes

String and slice beans. Heat oil in saucepan. Add chopped onion. If fresh meat is used, add now and stir. If cooked minced meat is used, add after 10 minutes or so with tomato sauce diluted in a little water, or chopped fresh tomatoes. Add water to cover, salt and pepper and cook gently for about half an hour. The same recipe can be used with a variety of vegetables, e.g. broad beans, fresh celery, fresh peas and fresh cauliflower.

PATATES SLİKME

(POT-FRIED POTATOES)

1 lb small potatoes   1–2 hours

2 cups oil

Peel the small, round potatoes, wash and dry. Pierce with a knife in three places. Put oil in a saucepan and lower heat. Toss the potatoes every so often, keeping the lid of the saucepan on. When they are golden, you can serve with a meat or chicken dish. Locally they are eaten alone as a main dish with a green salad.

KAYNANMIS KABAK

(BOILED COURGETTES)

SERVED COLD AS SALAD

1 lb courgettes   Serves 2–3 people

Wash, slice, and quarter courgettes and put into a saucepan of boiling salted water. Cook for about 10 to 15 minutes. Drain, place on a dish, dress with lemon juice and olive oil. Serve cold as salad.

KAVRILMIŞ KABAK

(COURGETTES FRIED)

½ hour

Courgettes can also be cut in thin slices lengthways, fried in hot oil and served cold with yogurt sauce, as a side dish.

İMAM BAYALDI

(FRIED AUBERGINES)

2 aubergines   ½ hour

Salt

Oil

Fresh tomatoes or tomato puree

1 teaspoon vinegar

Juice of 1 lemon

This is a well known dish and the translation of its name means 'the Imam fainted'. (The legend behind this name is that the Imam fainted because he couldn't digest the amount of oil which is needed to fry aubergines.)

Wash aubergines and cut the tops off. Slice in thin slices lengthways and sprinkle with salt. Lay out on a tea cloth to absorb moisture and thus prevent spitting. Then fry both sides until golden brown. Drain the oil from the frying pan, leaving about 2 tablespoons in the pan. Into this put either fresh tomatoes or tomato sauce and 1 teaspoon of vinegar. Cook for a few minutes, then pour over the aubergines. Add the juice of one lemon and serve cold as a side dish.

KAVRILMIŞ PATLICAN VE BİBER

(FRIED GREEN PEPPERS AND AUBERGINES)

½ hour

Wash and dry the peppers and slice them in half lengthways. Fry the aubergines, then the peppers, and pour tomato sauce over both.

KAYNANMIŞ BÖYRÜLCE

(BLACK EYED BEANS)

1 cup black-eyed beans

1 hour

1 teaspoon salt

Juice of one lemon

1 tablespoon olive oil

Soak beans overnight in cold water. Next morning pour away the water, put beans in a pan, cover with fresh water and cook for one hour or until beans are tender. While the beans are cooking, add the salt and a squeeze of lemon juice as this prevents them from going black. When they are tender drain, and throw away the water. Just before serving, add lemon juice and olive oil. This makes a delicious salad, or on hot days a meal in itself. It can be varied by cooking a few sticks of celery or young beet shoots with the beans, or by serving with rings of raw onions and slices of fresh tomatoes.

KURU PAKLA

(DRIED BROAD BEANS)

½ lb broad beans   1 hour

1 teaspoon salt

2 tablespoons vinegar

2 tablespoons olive oil

Wash broad beans and put into a saucepan. Cover with cold water and boil. From time to time add cold water as this helps to tenderize the beans. When tender, drain, add dressing of salt, vinegar and olive oil and serve cold.

TAZE PAKLA

(FRESH [OR FROZEN] BROAD BEANS)

Beans   20 minutes

Vinegar

Olive oil

If fresh beans are used, wash and string. If tough, use only the beans but if young, use the pods as well. Put into salted boiling water and cook. Serve dressed with vinegar and olive oil. Garnish with spring onions and green olives.

İNGİNAR

(GLOBE ARTICHOKES)

Artichokes   ½ hour

Vinegar

Wash and take off coarse outer leaves. Put water and vinegar into a saucepan and cook for about half an hour. When tender, drain and serve with lemon or vinegar dressing.

FASULYA

(DRIED BUTTER BEANS)

Beans   1 hour

Lemon juice   Olive oil

Soak beans overnight. Next morning wash, cover with cold water, add salt, and cook until tender. Then drain, and dress with lemon juice and olive oil. Garnish with finely chopped parsley and raw onion rings.

PATATES VE YUMURTA SALATA

(POTATO AND EGG SALAD)

20 minutes

Potatoes   Eggs

Onions   Parsley

Olive oil   Lemon juice

Boil potatoes and slice into rings. Hard boil eggs and slice. Arrange both on a dish, garnish with parsley and onion rings. Dress with lemon juice and olive oil.

YOGURT SALATA

(YOGURT SALAD)

1–2 hours

Yogurt   Olive oil

Put yogurt in a muslin, and pass it through until all moisture is lost. Make round balls and serve with a little olive oil.

SALATA

(RAW SALADS)

Salads of lettuce, cucumber, or tomatoes are the same

everywhere, except that we put a lemon and oil dressing over them and use chopped onions, finely chopped parsley and black or green olives for garnishing.

SARMALAHANA SALATA

(CABBAGE SALAD)

White Cabbage	Salt
Juice of 1 lemon	Olive oil
1 tangerine	

Shred white cabbage very finely. Add juice of 1 lemon. 1 tangerine and salt. Add olive oil and serve as salad.

EKŞİLİ ZEYTUN

(OLIVES SERVED AS SALAD)

Often black or green olives are served as a salad with a lemon, and tangerine and oil dressing.

PİLAKÎ

A great favourite in Turkey is cold cooked vegetables in olive oil, served as side dishes. This is peculiar to Turkey rather than Cyprus.

TAZE FASULYA (SOĞUK)

(FRESH GREEN BEANS)

1 hour

1 lb green beans

3 fresh tomatoes

3 tablespoons olive oil

Salt

1 onion

Wash and string the beans and put into a saucepan with the olive oil and the finely chopped onions and tomatoes. Saute for a few minutes, then add salt and enough water to cover the vegetables. Put on the lid and allow to cook gently for about one hour. Serve cold.

PRATSA PİLAKÎ

(PILAKI OF LEEKS)

¾ hour

1 lb leeks

3 tablespoons olive oil

few carrots

3 cups water

1 tablespoon rice

3 tomatoes

salt and black pepper

Wash leeks and cut into 2-inch long pieces. Wash and chop up carrots. Put the oil into a saucepan, add vegetables, heat and stir. Then add water, salt and black pepper and cook gently about ¾ of an hour. Serve cold.

LAHANA DOLDURMA

(STUFFED CABBAGE [COLD])

½ hour

1 cabbage	1 lb rice
4 oz corn oil	2 oz sultanas
2 oz almonds	2 cups water

Wash a cabbage and chop off the roots. Bring water to the boil in a saucepan and dip the cabbage in until well submerged for a few minutes. Take out and put on a dish to cool. Prepare the rice filling as follows: Warm the oil and add chopped and blanched almonds. When slightly pink, add the rice. Stir once or twice and add two cups of water and sultanas. When all the water is absorbed, remove the pan from the stove, scoop out the middle of the cabbage and fill it with the partially cooked rice. Also put a spoonful of rice between each leaf. Tie the cabbage with a string. Put two tablespoons of oil into a saucepan and when hot, drop the cabbage into it. Then add two cups of water and boil gently. When cooked, let it cool before removing from the pan. Cut into slices and serve cold.

KABAK YÄHNI

(COURGETTE RATATOUILLE)

1 lb of courgettes	2 fresh tomatoes or tinned tomatoes
½ cup of oil	1 tblsp. of dried mint
1 large onion	seasoning

35

Cut courgettes into one-inch pieces. Chop up the onion and cook slightly in oil, using a saucepan. Then add the courgettes and tomatoes into this. Add very little water as courgettes produce water as they cook. Add to this the dried mint, and cook gently on slow fire for half an hour. Serve cold, with more dried mint if wanted.

İNGİNAR YEMEĞİ

(ARTICHOKE HEADS)

4 artichokes   ½ hour

½ lb small onions

½ lb small potatoes

3 tablespoons olive oil

salt and pepper

Clean the artichokes and take off all the leaves and the furry bit in the centre. Put the hearts on a baking dish. Clean the onions and put them whole between the artichokes. Then clean the potatoes and put on top. Add one cup of water, olive oil, salt and pepper. Cook in a medium oven for ½ an hour or until the vegetables are tender. Serve cold.

DOLMA

(STUFFED VINE LEAVES)
½ to ¾ hours

This is one of those delicacies which people love but think

that it's too hard to do oneself. Apart from rolling the vine leaves, there is nothing to it. You will need:

1 lb minced meat	Parsley
¼ cup rice	½ lb vine leaves
1 Onion	1 tablespoon oil
4 tomatoes	Juice of ½ lemon
salt	

Take a basin, put the vine leaves into it (If tinned pour boiling water over them.) and leave for half an hour. If fresh boil them until the stalks can be removed easily. Take another bowl and into this put the raw mince and rice, finely chopped onions, parsley, salt and pepper to taste, and chopped tomatoes. Stir all together. Now comes the difficult part: take a vine leaf, spread it on the palm of your hand, or put it on a saucer. Now put a little of the mixture on it and fold each end, then bring the top end down and roll into a sausage rather loosely to allow for cooking. If leaves are too small you can have two to make one large one. Put it all in a row at the bottom of a saucepan. Add water, about two cups, add lemon juice and oil. Place a saucer on top of the dolmas to prevent them from opening. Put the lid of the saucepan on, bring up to boil and simmer gently for about half an hour.

Local wines are delicious when you can savour them in the locality; and Turkey has a whole range of wines — red, pink or white — ranging from dry to sweet, which can be matched up with the food: red wines with meat, white wines with fish, and rosé wines when you are not sure.

But the vegetable dishes of Turkey do not fall into such neat compartments. So, when choosing wine to go with them, you can also try something new — contrasting tastes.

With the richer dishes like the moussakas or the bastıs, you could serve a light red wine with a refreshing acidity, like Buzbağ (the French equivalent of this would be Medoc or Beaujolais).

Again, just as you serve the crisp contrasts of radishes or salads with these dishes, so you could try a light white wine like Kavaklidere (or its western equivalents, such as a dry Hock like Liebfraumilch Kellergeist, or a good white Burgundy such as Domaine de Beauregard Pouilly Fuissé).

And you will find that many of the rosé wines harmonise most attractively with Turkish vegetable dishes; there is a Portuguese wine with more flavour than most, and a hint of a sparkle, called Santos Rosé, which comes in most attractive stoneware pitchers which seem to fit particularly well with gay and informal Turkish meals.

Fish

Cyprus, in spite of being an island, has a very limited variety of fish. Red and grey mullet are the most popular. One sees their nets pulled in all along the sea-shore. With strings of fish in their hands, they knock at doors, wanting to know if you would like some fish, very like the 'onion men' over here. But, my word, that fish tastes good.

On the other hand, Turkey has an endless variety of fish. Very popular, of course, is sword fish cooked on skewers. But the seas must be so full of fish that even an amateur, after a day's fishing off the Islands, will come home with any number of halibut or turbot. Most boys go in for sea-fishing as it is a very popular sport.

The sword fish was highly prized in Tudor times, when Evliya Chelebi wrote describing how it was caught. 'In front of the Village (Beykoz) is a dalyan (wooden platform) for trapping sword fish. This platform consists of five or six poles on top of which sits a man who keeps a look-out for the fish that come down from the Black Sea. When he sees them drawing near, he throws a stone into the sea to scare them, which causes all the fish to make for the bay, and thus swim straight into the nets laid for them under the water. The nets are closed on the warning from the look-out, and the fishermen crowd round to kill the fish whose swords are now powerless to offer resistance. This fish, if boiled with garlic and vine leaves, is excellent.'

Describing another part of Istanbul he says: 'Close by is the Walk of Kiamish, frequented by those who are fond of fishing for Kia-balığı (Grayling) which are only to be found in this spot. This fish, though black and lustreless, is very tasty and has no smell, nor does it cause indigestion however much one may eat of it.' And I cannot help wondering whether it was a recommendation or a warning when he wrote: 'At Tersane harbour Sultan Ibrahim built a pavilion by the sea-shore which may be compared to the Palace of Khavarnak (a mythical Persian palace). Here they catch oysters which are eaten with lemon and washed down with wine. People who eat oysters without wine will find them a powerful aphrodisiac.'

Other fish to be found in different parts of Turkey are Sea Bream, Tunny Fish, Lobster and Shrimp.

BURBAN BALIK

(FRIED RED OR GREY MULLET)

15 minutes

This fish not only tastes good but looks good as well.

40

Fish   Oil

Flour   Slices of fresh lemon

Wash the fish. Then dip lightly in seasoned flour and fry in
hot fat. Serve with slices of fresh lemon.

BALIK SALATA

(FISH SALAD)

15 minutes

This is also very popular. Usually a meaty kind of fish is
chosen.

Steaks or whole fish

1 lemon

Olive oil dressing

Parsley

Boil steaks or whole fish. Cool. Dress with a lemon and
olive oil dressing. Just before serving, sprinkle with finely
chopped parsley.

BALIK KEBABI

(FISH KEBAB)

For this choose small fish.   15—20 minutes

Small fish

Vine leaves

Olive oil

Wash and salt the fish. Wash and grease vine leaves with a little olive oil. Wrap a fish in each of these and cook gently on charcoal. When cooked, remove vine leaves as these are only used to give the fish a subtle flavour.

BALIK PİLAKÎ

(FISH PILAKI)

¾ hour

Fish that can be filleted, e.g., cod or halibut, is used for this recipe.

Fillet of cod or halibut

1 lemon

Potatoes

Parsley

1 teaspoon salt

3 fresh tomatoes

½ cup oil

½ cup water

Wash fish and place in a baking dish. Cover with peeled and finely sliced lemon and then a layer of sliced potatoes. To this add finely chopped parsley, a teaspoon of salt, and three fresh tomatoes, sliced. Lastly, add ½ cup of oil and ½ cup of water, and bake in a medium oven for about three-quarters of an hour. Serve cold.

TALATURLU BALIK

(DRESSED FISH)

7 minutes

1 lb haddock

¼ tahini

Juice of 1 lemon

Garlic salt

4 oz ground walnuts

Put the haddock to cook in boiling salted water for 7 minutes. When tender, remove all obvious bones. Put on a serving dish and allow to cool.

Mix the tahini with a little water alternating with lemon juice until the mixture is creamy. Add garlic salt to taste and the ground walnuts. Mix well and pour over the fish. Decorate the top with finely chopped parsley, red pepper, and a few drops of olive oil before serving.

TALATUR

(FISH SAUCE)

This can be used with fried, steamed or baked fish.

¼ lb walnuts

Juice of 1 or 2 lemons

Olive oil

Grind the walnuts into fairly small pieces BUT DO NOT POWDER. Mix them with the juice of one or two lemons, according to size, and a few drops of olive oil.

This sauce is then poured over the fish and decorated with finely chopped parsley.

FISH COURSE WINES

If you are trying to escape from the tradition of white wine with fish, why not try rosé wine with Red Mullet? The colour harmony is fascinating. For my own taste, I would choose Tavel Rosé, or else Eperon Rosé from Bordeaux; but if you prefer something a little less dry, perhaps Anniversary Anjou Rosé or Cabernet Rosé would be to your taste.

With the fish salad and the cold fish pie (pilakî), I would prefer white wine, either a light medium-dry wine like Güzel Marmara from vineyards not far from Istanbul (this would be parallel to a Graves or a Riesling wine) or a Semillon Sekşarap — dry wine from the Semillon grape variety — which might be replaced by a white Burgundy, especially with fish dressed with Talatur sauce, notably a fine full wine from Chassagne Montrachet.

Poultry

'The Sergeant's bus is coming. Hurry!' is the cry every Friday. It's Market Day. People from neighbouring villages are all rushing to town to sell their goods. 'The Sergeant' is the local bus driver. He is quite a character — constantly making remarks like 'Come on, Ma! Have you tied a red ribbon round your hens? They must look pretty on market day!' And with legs tied together, these cackling hens are not fat and self-satisfied like battery hens. They are thin and gawky as they have to scratch for a living. Most days the bus is full of passengers and the cautious or experienced ones look under the seats before choosing a place, and watch the uninitiated having their ankles snipped! The hens travelling under the seat or on the roof of the bus, complain from time to time of their fate.

Market Day is quite something; everyone arguing and bargaining, feeling the goods for freshness, scolding the men for dishonesty, feeling the hens for fatness, looking for bright eyes in the fish. Further down the street, Lokmas are being fried and sold at so much a dozen. They are very popular — a bit like doughnuts only much smaller in size. At another stall they are cleaning prickly pears invitingly with gloved hands, as even the experienced do not handle these with bare hands. It's quite normal for someone to say, 'Please clean a few dozen and I'll eat them here.'

Ordinary shopping becomes quite tame after shopping at a market.

KAVRULMUŞ TAVUK

(FRIED CHICKEN)

15—20 minutes

If the chicken is young, it is almost always served fried with a rice pilaff mixed with nuts and raisins. The chicken is first washed and cut into pieces, then rubbed with lemon juice and fried. The pilaff is prepared as follows:

BADEMLİ ÜZÜMLÜ PİLAV

(RICH PILAFF)

1 cup rice

2 ozs margarine

4 ozs blanched almonds

1½ cups broth

½ teaspoon salt

2 ozs sultanas

Wash and blanche the rice at least half-an-hour before cooking. Put the margarine into a saucepan, add the blanched almonds and fry until slightly pink. Then add the broth and bring to the boil. Drain the rice and add it also with the salt and sultanas. Leave to cook slowly until the broth is all absorbed, switch off the heat, and cover with a towel or teacloth. Serve when required.

CHERKEZ TAVUK

(CIRCASSIAN CHICKEN)

1 hour

This recipe is for boilers:
Cook the hen and remove the bones. Cut the meat into neat portions and keep warm while making the sauce as follows:

2 cups broth

Thick slice of bread

¼ lb walnuts

Clove of garlic

Grate the bread and grind the walnuts. Boil the broth and add the grated breadcrumbs and ground walnuts, salt and garlic. Cook this slowly until it becomes like a thick gravy. Pour over the chicken and serve with a plain rice pilaff as a base. Decorate it with paprika.

HİNDİ

(TURKEY)

15 minutes

Make the stuffing for a roast turkey in the following way:

2 ozs blanched almonds

2 ozs margarine

Turkey's liver

2 ozs sultanas

1 cup rice

1 cup broth

Chop up the turkey liver finely. Put the margarine into a saucepan, add the liver, blanched almonds, and sultanas. Stir once or twice, and add the rice and the broth. Cook until the broth is absorbed. Stuff and roast the turkey in the normal way, and serve with a rice pilaff mixed with pine nuts and raisins.

MAKARINA
(MACARONI CHEESE)

Macaroni   20 minutes

1 teaspoon salt

2 oz hard cheese

Dried mint

Boilers are done in a pressure cooker with an onion and salt for about three-quarters of an hour, according to size and age. With this you can serve a macaroni cheese made in the following way:

Remove the hen from the pressure cooker and bring the remaining broth up to the boil. Add the salt. Break up macaroni into 2—3 inch pieces and add to the boiling broth. Cover and cook for 10 minutes. Grate a hard cheese and add a little dried mint to it. Sprinkle it on top of the drained macaroni and serve with the boiled chicken.

WINE AND POULTRY

Most wines go well with poultry: red and róse wines are perhaps a little more suitable for fried chicken and roast turkey and I personally would prefer a white wine with boiled chicken. The delicate flavour and rich sauce of Cherkez Tavuk seems to call for quite a full rich white wine, and if a suitable Turkish wine were not available, it might be interesting to try a Russian wine — after all, the dish has Circassian origins.

Meat Dishes and Kebabs

East of Turkey, great plateaux stretch almost endlessly to Lake Baykal. For many centuries, generation after generation of nomadic tribes have boiled over from the cauldron of races to be found here and have poured destructively into the fertile lands around. Among these tribes were the earliest ancestors of the Turks.

These roaming people, accustomed to the saddle from the moment they were born, drawn or driven always westwards, were soon separated from their flocks and family cooking pots and had to learn to live off the land.

Thus was born perhaps the most typical style of Turkish meat cooking (Kebab). These tribal bands, pausing only to fight, to feed and to sleep, had no time for the finesse of cooking with utensils. We can picture them coming upon a flock, hungry and weary from the fight. How gladly they must have reined in their horses and slain the sheep with their knives. A fire would have been hastily built and pieces of meat, carefully skewered onto swords, roasted as if on a spit and eagerly devoured.

Time passed and the Turks became masters of a mighty empire, but one of the nomadic traditions which they never forgot, even in the elegance of their palaces, was this style of cooking. Refined as the Kebab has become since its rude beginnings, in spirit it has never changed; instead of a hasty camp fire, the carefully-attended charcoal grill; in place of the heavy and curving sword, the more suitable skewer. The tender flesh of sucking lambs, carefully prepared and seasoned with onions and herbs, has taken the place of the swiftly-butchered animals.

Nowadays, the Turkish housewife takes advantage of the most modern methods of cookery, such as electricity and gas, but anyone who has enjoyed the subtle flavour of smoke in meat will understand why leading chefs the world over still take the trouble to cook Kebab over charcoal. You can capture a similar flavour by seasoning the meat with Hickory smoked salt.

Until recently the Kebab was unknown in the west, except by Scouts. However, this situation is rapidly changing and the Kebab style of cooking has been established.

Here are a few traditional Kebab recipes:

52

ŞİŞ KEBAB

(MEAT ON A SKEWER)

15—20 min.

Lamb fillets
or
a piece off the leg of lamb

1 onion

Parsley

2 tomatoes

1 tblsp. of
olive oil

Chop up the meat into one-inch squares. Sprinkle with olive oil, and cover the meat with tin foil and leave for half an hour. This helps to tenderise the meat. Put the pieces on a skewer and cook on a charcoal grill. Salt, after the meat has been cooked.

Serve with finely chopped raw onions and fresh parsley with slices of cucumber and tomatoes and a squeeze of lemon juice.

ŞAŞLIK
(pronounced 'Shashlik'.)

(MEAT ALTERNATING WITH VEGETABLES)

20 minutes

Lamb fillets

1 kidney

Tomatoes

Onions

Mushrooms

Green peppers

Chop up the meat, kidney and all the vegetables. Put the

pieces on a skewer, alternating meat and vegetables. Cook on charcoal grill. Serve with chopped parsley, onion, cucumber and tomato salad.

CİĞER KEBAB

(LIVER KEBAB)

½ lb liver   15—20 minutes

1 kidney

Cut liver into one-inch pieces, salt it and put it on a skewer. A few slices of chopped kidney can be added. Cook either under a slow grill or on a barbecue. Serve with raw chopped onions, parsley, tomatoes and lemon juice.

STEWS

Turkish stews are cooked in liquid oil (ground nut oil, for example, or corn oil).

BASTI

(STEW)

2 lbs leeks   1 hour

1 lb scrag-end of mutton

3—4 tomatoes

1 teaspoon vinegar

54

Salt and pepper

3 cups of water

Black pepper

Wash and chop up leeks into one-inch pieces. Put the leeks into a saucepan with the fat and stir once or twice with a wooden spoon. Add meat, tomatoes, vinegar, salt, pepper and water. Cook on a low heat for about one hour. Serve with a crushed wheat pilaff and have raw radishes as a side-dish.

FIRINDA CİĞER

(LIVER CASSEROLE)

1—2 hours

1 lb lamb's liver	Flour
3 onions	Black pepper
½ cup red wine	White pepper

Chop liver into thin slices, dip into seasoned flour, fry lightly, then put into a casserole. Add 3 fried onions in rings and ½ cup of red wine with some water and some black and white pepper. Cook slowly for 1½ hours. Serve with mashed potatoes.

FIRINDA TAVŞAN

(BRAISED RABBIT)

Medium-sized rabbit

1½ hours

1 lemon

4 or 5 onions

Salt and pepper

Cooking wine if required

Wash rabbit and cut into portions. Rub with a fresh lemon to make skin whiter. Fry lightly and put into a casserole. Add fried onions, a little red cooking wine (about ½ cup), ½ cup of water, salt and pepper. Cook for 1½ hours in a slow oven.

SILGIÇ

(SHOULDER OF LAMB [POT-ROAST])

Joint of shoulder of lamb   ¾ hour

Chop up the meat into portions, add salt and one cup of water. Cook slowly until the meat is tender and the water is all absorbed. Remove all the bone from the meat, put it back into the saucepan, add a little water and cook on a very slow heat until the water is absorbed and the meat cooks in its own fat. Serve this with roast potatoes and a green salad.

OMUZ DOLDURMASI

(STUFFED SHOULDER)

2—3 hours according to size

Rice pilaff with pine nuts [see page 49]

Joint of shoulder of lamb

Ask the butcher to prepare the joint for stuffing. Stuff under the shoulder blade with the cooked pilaff and sew it up. Then roast the joint as you would normally. Serve with vegetables.

TAVA

(POT ROAST)

1 hour

1 lb mutton	1 lb potatoes
2 lbs onions	Oil
3 tomatoes	Cumin

Cut the meat into small pieces and boil in salted water until they are tender. Saute chopped onions in oil until pink and add the meat with chopped-up potatoes and tomatoes. Cook all together. Sprinkle with cumin and serve. This dish is very good on cold days.

KAVRULMUŞ KIYMA

(COOKED MINCED MEAT)

15—20 minutes

Minced meat   Onion

Parsley   Salt and pepper

Cooked minced meat is the basis for most stews, and fillings for vegetables and for some pastry dishes. It is best cooked in oil with chopped parsley and onion, salt and pepper. Stir it, then add water. Cook until all the water and the oil has been absorbed.

KADIN BUDU or KÖFTES

(TURKISH RISSOLES)

½ hour

1 lb minced meat   1 egg

¼ cup rice   Salt and pepper

Parsley   Olive oil

[Kadin budu means 'woman's thighs'.]

Boil rice until soft, drain and stir in the meat. Add salt and pepper. Let the mixture cool, then add finely chopped parsley. Make into croquettes, dip these into beaten egg and fry in hot fat until golden. Pierce with a skewer to make sure the middle is cooked. Do not turn the köftes in hot fat too many times, as they are liable to crumble. Allow one side to cook and then roll it on to the other side. Serve with chips.

SUMMAKLI KÖFTE

(LITTLE MEAT BALLS SPICED WITH SUMACK)

½ hour

1 lb minced meat	salt and pepper
2 medium potatoes	Oil
1 small onion	

Grate the potatoes and onion on to the minced meat and add salt and pepper. Knead well together. Make into round balls and fry in hot fat until brown. Serve on toasted bread. Pour beaten yogurt over it and sprinkle with Sumak. The toast can be moistened with a little broth if desired.

This mixture can be served with a tomato sauce instead of yogurt.

TOMATO SAUCE

10-15 minutes

1 tablespoon melted fat

2 tablespoons tomato sauce or tomato puree

1 cup of water

Boil these ingredients together and add the köftes. Continue boiling on a low gas until all the juice is absorbed.

ŞİŞ KÖFTE

(RISSOLE KEBAB)

15-20 minutes

1 lb minced meat

1 large slice of stale bread

Salt and pepper

1 medium onion

Grate the stale bread into a bowl and add the minced meat, salt, pepper and grated onion. Knead together. Press a little of this mixture on to the middle of a skewer. Grill and serve with chopped parsley, chopped raw onions and lemon juice.

The same mixture can be made into round shapes and cooked on a charcoal grill like Wimpies and served with hot rolls. This makes a delicious snack.

PATATES MUSAKASI

(MOUSSAKA OF POTATOES)

¾ - 1 hour

1 lb potatoes

3 onions

½ lb cooked minced meat

Parsley

Seasoning

1 tablespoon tomato sauce

Peel and wash potatoes and slice in rounds. Dry and fry slightly. Wash, slice and fry the onions slightly. Place potatoes, onions and cooked minced meat in layers in a casserole, finishing with mince on top. Add water mixed with tomato sauce and seasoning and cook gently for about one hour or less in a medium oven. Serve with a green salad.

KOLAKAZ MUSAKKA

(MOUSSAKA OF YAM)

½ hour

2 lbs of yam	2 onions
1 cup of oil	Juice of one lemon
½ lb of tomatoes	

½ lb of cooked minced meat

Peel a root of Yam and slice it into rounds of ¼ inch thick. Brown these in oil. Put one layer into a saucepan. Spread a layer of cooked minced meat on top, alternating it with layers of yam. Add either fresh or tinned tomatoes, lemon juice and seasoning. Add enough water to cover the yam and cook for half an hour.

PATLICAN MUSAKASI

(MOUSSAKA OF AUBERGINES)

3 aubergines	1 hour
1 lb potatoes	½ lb cooked minced meat
3 onions	Parsley
½ lb tomatoes	Seasoning

Wash and peel aubergines, partly slice and quarter. Fry slightly in hot fat. Do the same as for the previous recipe, only adding the aubergines to the layers of potatoes, onions and minced meat. Instead of tomato sauce, add a layer of fresh tomatoes, cut up, and parsley.

KABAK MUSAKASI

(MOUSSAKA OF COURGETTES)

1 hour

This is done in the same way, only slice courgettes in rings and use plenty of fresh parsley, both in the minced meat and in the moussaka.

KUŞ BAŞI

(CUBES OF MEAT POT-ROASTED)

1 lb mutton	¾ hour
1 onion	¼ cup of oil
3 or 4 tomatoes	1 teaspoonful salt
2 lbs potatoes	3 tablespoons fat

Cut up the meat into small pieces. Put them into a saucepan with the chopped onion and tomatoes, salt, one tablespoon of oil and enough water to cover. Cook slowly until the water is all absorbed and the meat is tender. Then chop the potatoes into small pieces, fry them and add them to the meat. Add 2 more tablespoons of oil and cook gently all together. Serve hot with a green salad, or on a bed of plain rice pilaff.

KADIN PARMAĞI

(GIRLS' FINGERS)

½ hour

½ lb minced meat	Salt
2 onions	Pepper
Parsley	2 cups flour

Filling:

Fry the minced meat with chopped onions and parsley in a little fat. Add water and cook until the water is absorbed and meat is tender. Add salt and pepper.

Make pastry with 2 cups of flour and ¾ of a cup of water. Sieve the flour and add water gradually, making a soft dough. You may not need to use all the water. Roll out the pastry into 2 inch squares and put the filling in. Roll as if you were rolling a cigarette, and twist the ends. Then fry in hot fat and serve with a plain yogurt dressing, decorated with a sprinkle of red pepper.

BÖREK

(MEAT PASTIES)

½ hour

Cut the pastry into slightly larger squares and fill with minced meat filling, prepared as for Kadın Parmağı. Fold diagonally and stick the ends together with water. These pies should be baked in a medium oven, temp.350, for about half an hour. If the pastry is freshly made, they can be fried.

The same recipe can have a spinach filling instead of meat:

(SPINACH PASTIES)

1 lb spinach	¼ cup rice
3 ozs.fat	20 ozs. sultanas

Wash and chop the spinach. Heat the fat in a pan and add the spinach, stirring all the time. Add a little water, rice and sultanas. When the rice is partially cooked, allow the mixture to cool and use as a filling for the pastry. Cook as the meat pies.

LAHMACUN

(PIZZA OR TART)

½ hour

Dough	Mixture
1 teaspoonful dried yeast	½ lb minced meat
1 teaspoonful sugar	2 or 3 onions
2 cups of flour	Salt and pepper
	½ lb fresh tomatoes
	2 ozs. nuts
	2 tablespoons olive oil

Dough:

Mix the dried yeast and the sugar with a little warm water and allow to rise. When it is full of bubbles, it is ready to be used. Sieve the flour into a bowl, add the yeast and a little more water. Knead into a soft dough. Leave in a warm place for one hour.

Mixture:

Add the finely chopped onions, salt and pepper to taste, cut-up tomatoes, a few chopped nuts and the olive oil. Mix it all together.

When the dough is ready, roll out into thin rounds and grease each round with a little olive oil. Spread the meat mixture very thinly on these rounds. Place them on greased baking trays and cook in the oven for about fifteen minutes. Serve with quarters of fresh lemon.

LALANGI

(RABBIT IN BATTER)

Medium-size rabbit   ¾ hour

Juice of ½ lemon

½ pint of batter

Oil

Wash rabbit and chop into large pieces. Cook with salt, lemon juice and enough water to cover (about half-an-hour or until meat is really tender). The addition of lemon helps to whiten the meat. Remove the meat from the bones and cut into smaller portions. Make batter with flour, egg and water, and dip each piece of meat into it. Fry in hot fat until golden brown.

WINES FOR TURKISH MEAT DISHES

One of the joys of Turkish cooking is that almost any sound, flavoury wine tastes good with it. If you are in Turkey, the leading hotels will give you a considerable choice, but elsewhere you will probably drink the local wine, and almost certainly enjoy it. Even the roughest village wines such as one used to find in some of the mountain coffee shops of Cyprus taste refreshingly delicious when mixed with fizzy lemonade. The dedicated gastronome might throw up his hands in horror thinking of the scorn poured upon port and lemon, but I challenge him to taste red wine and lemon in the open air, shaded by an arbour of grape vines. Drink it with kebabs grilled over charcoal, accompanied by cool salad dressed with lemon juice — and if you have a taste for the off-beat, choose an arbour shaded by gourds or loofahs, where the pendant fruits form strange patterns of light and shade.

This type of meal could also be accompanied by a light Bordeaux or Claret, a Médoc or St Julien. Burgundies would be better suited to the dishes where meat and vegetables are stewed together, forming a rich gravy of their mingled flavours.

Sometimes, Turkish meat dishes are served with yogurt, such as spinach and beet in chapter 3. Here a medium-dry white wine from Bordeaux (Eperon d'Or Graves or Entre-deux-Mers) or from Germany (Niersteiner Domtal or Liebfraumilch Blackfriars) would seem well chosen.

If you are enjoying your wine, why not serve cheese immediately after the meat course, as these wines go well with cheese. Thus the sweet course will either be accompanied by a rich sweet wine or by Turkish coffee.

Jams and Sweetmeats

I often tell stories to my children of the way we lived and the type of food we ate when we were young. They sit and listen fascinated as if I am telling them a fairy story of another world. And yet it's barely 35 years ago that all this happened.

We lived in Cyprus then, where the sun shone most of the time (that fact alone is a phenomenon to them), where there was someone in the kitchen all the time and where there was always excitement and bustle when someone's favourite dish was being prepared. If it was summer and fresh fruit was in season, we often saw mother making cherry jam — with lovely juicy red cherries, pipping each one with a hair-pin, then leaving it in lime to harden. Plums, fresh walnuts and peaches were all given the same treatment. There was something happening every day, until all our pots were filled and stored away.

And when it was blossom time, the house and garden were filled with the perfume of orange blossom and roses being distilled. We used to use this water to clean our faces as Mother used to say it would make our skin soft. How right she was. Never use ordinary water.

One of my favourite jams was made with orange peel. I still make it in my little kitchen in Hampstead, and even now, as I cook this jam, I see orchards full of white blossom, filling the air with its heavy scent.

I wonder whether we shall ever regain the lost art of the kitchen, or whether our grandchildren will just take a few tablets and carry on with their busy lives without stopping, in order to keep up with the ever increasing speed of modern times.

TATLILAR

(SWEETMEATS)

Puddings, as known in the West, do not exist in Turkey, except the occasional stewed fruits, and milk puddings such as mahallebi (which is similar to blancmange) and rice pudding. Most meals end with fresh fruit, of which there is an abundance. Sweetmeats are made when there is a special occasion, or during Bayrams, which are feast days. These sweetmeats can be divided into three classes — those made out of pastry, the ones made out of semolina and the ones made with yeast. All these are of course dipped into cold syrup which gives them richness and a honey flavour. As there are large quantities of nuts, the fillings of sweetmeats are always ground nuts of some kind.

There is a great tradition of hospitality among Turks and when visitors arrive unexpectedly, they are offered Turkish coffee or sweetmeats or fruits preserved in syrup. These are usually preserved when cherries, walnuts, apricots, peaches, dates or any other suitable fruits are in season.

I have given only a few recipes for these as they take rather a long time to prepare and the idea of this book was not only to introduce the Turkish way of cooking, but also easily prepared recipes.

ŞURUPLU TATLILAR

(SYRUP FOR TURKISH PASTRIES)

1 lb sugar	2 glasses sugar
or	
1 glass water	1 glass water

Boil up until syrupy, so that it drips slowly off the spoon. Let it cool before using.

The main thing to remember about pastries is that the hot pastries are dropped into cold syrup, so that the sugar is absorbed into the pastry.

EKMEK KADEYİF (1)

(PALACE BREAD)

1 packet Scotch pancakes   ½ hour

2 eggs

2 cups frying oil

¼ lb walnuts

½ pint double cream (whipped)

Dip pancakes into the beaten egg, fry in hot oil and drop into cold syrup; when serving sprinkle with ground walnuts and some whipped cream.

Scotch pancakes are substitutes for special dried bread which cannot be obtained in this country. If, however, you can get hold of some of the proper ingredient, see the next recipe.

EKMEK KADEYİF (2)

1 hour

In the previous recipe I gave a substitute material for the real thing. Just in case you visit Turkey or Cyprus and can bring back Ekmek Kadeyif, here is the real recipe. Ekmek Kadeyif looks like a well-baked crust of bread. It is normally sold in two rounds. But do not attempt to cook all at once unless you have about 30 guests to dinner as it enlarges and expands when soaked.

Put the Ekmek Kadeyif in an aluminium or copper tray twice the size of the ingredient. Pour boiling water over it and leave until all the water has been absorbed. Now prepare a heavy syrup, by boiling 2 lbs. of sugar and one cup of water together. When this has come to the boil, pour it over the Kadeyif and place the tray on a slow heat. Basting it continually, cook gently for about an hour until all the syrup has been absorbed. Then cut it into squares and place it on a serving dish. Sprinkle the top with chopped walnuts and thick cream. Just before serving, add a drop of brandy on top of each square.

SÜTLÜ BÖREK

(MILK PASTRY)

1 cup semolina   ½ hour

1 pint milk

syrup made from ½ lb of sugar

1 lb flaky pastry

Cook the semolina with the milk until it looks like cold semolina pudding. Roll out the flaky pastry into 4 inch squares. Put a spoonful of semolina mixture in the centre of each and stick the sides with water. Put on a greased tray and bake in a medium oven. When they are done, pour cold syrup over them and serve cold.

PAKLAVA

(PASTRY WITH NUTS IN SYRUP)

½ lb walnuts or almonds   1½ hours

1 lb sugar

1 tablespoon cinnamon

2 tablespoons sugar

1 lb ready-made Paklava pastry

¼ lb unsalted butter

1 glass water

Grind nuts and mix with cinnamon and sugar. Roll out the pastry layer by layer as thinly as possible, sprinkling a few drops of the melted butter over each layer before putting the next layer on top. When you get half way (i.e. if you are having 8 layers, when you get to the 4th layer) sprinkle the pastry thickly with the nut mixture. Continue this process until you have used all the layers, then cut into diamond shapes. Put on a greased tray and bake for 1½ hours in a slow oven. When pink, pour the cold syrup over it, which is made by boiling the sugar and the water until it thickens a little more than for other pastries and sweets.

Paklava pastry can be ordered from oriental stores or pastry shops.

ŞAMALİ

(SEMOLINA IN SYRUP)

½ - ¾ hour

4 cups semolina	Syrup:
2 cups sugar	3 cups sugar
1 tablespoon baking powder	1½ cups water
2 cups water	
1 tablespoon yogurt	

Prepare a standard Turkish syrup with 3 cups sugar to 1½ cups water, boil up and when it thickens take off the heat and allow to cool. Put the semolina, sugar and baking powder into a bowl and make a dough with the water. Grease a baking tray with tahini rather than fat. Pour the dough into the tray and glaze the top of the mixture with the beaten yogurt. Decorate the top with blanched almonds and put it into a medium oven. After 15 minutes remove the mixture from the oven and cut into strips with a wet knife. Put it back in the oven until it is cooked. Then pour the cold syrup over it and allow to cool.

PORTOKAL TATLISI

(ORANGE SWEET)

2 oranges	½ hour
2 cups sugar	
1 cup water	
1 carton double cream	
1 lemon	

Grate off the skins of the oranges and cook in enough water to cover them until the oranges feel tender when pierced by a skewer. This may take up to two hours of boiling but if a pressure cooker is used, 15 minutes is enough. When oranges are tender, put on a plate and slice them. Throw away the water they have been cooked in. Put the sugar and the water into another saucepan and bring to the boil. Add a squeeze of lemon and put the slices of oranges into it. Boil for about 15 minutes. When the syrup runs thickly off the spoon, switch off the heat. Allow to cool and serve with whipped cream on each slice.

PORTOKAL KABUĞU

(PRESERVE OF ORANGE PEEL)

4 oranges   1½ hours

2 cups sugar

1 cup water

1 carton double cream

Quarter an orange and remove the inside. Grate the peel and put it to soak in cold water for 24 hours. Next day, put fresh water into a saucepan and boil the peel for one hour (or 15 minutes in a pressure cooker). When soft, remove from heat. Mix the sugar and water together in a preserving pan and bring to the boil. Add the peel and cook together until there is a thick syrup. When cool, either serve with cream or on its own.

This is one of those recipes where you are using something, which in the normal way you would have thrown away — therefore it tastes doubly delicious!

KIZMEMESI KABUĞU

(PRESERVE OF GRAPEFRUIT PEEL)

1 grapefruit

2 cups sugar

1 cup water

(The Turkish for 'grapefruit' means 'girl's breast')

Quarter a grapefruit and remove the peel. Grate the outside of the peel (that is remove the zest partly). Leave it to soak in cold water for three days, changing the water every day. On the third day put fresh water in and boil it until soft. Now boil the sugar and water until it thickens slightly. Add the peel and cook slowly. When the syrup is thick, remove from heat, allow to cool and serve with thick cream.

ŞURUPLU SEFTALİ

(PEACHES)

1 lb peaches	15 minutes
2 lb sugar	
1½ cups water	
1 lemon	

Dip peaches in boiling water, cut in half and remove skins and stones gently without bruising the fruit. Soak the fruit for 24 hours in a weak lime solution. This hardens it so that it does not go too mushy in cooking. After 24 hours, boil the water and sugar and put the washed fruit into it. Simmer gently. Peel the lemon, cut into slices, and add to the boiling fruit. When syrup begins to thicken slightly, remove from heat. Allow to cool before serving.

KİRAZ REÇELİ

(WHOLE CHERRY JAM)

1 lb cherries	15 - 20 minutes

1 lb castor sugar

¼ cup water

Lemon juice

Slaked lime

Wash the cherries and remove the stalks. Soak in water mixed with lime (to the consistency of thin cream) for one hour to make the fruit hard. Then wash the cherries again and remove the stones. Put them with the sugar in a saucepan and add water. Stir from time to time and bring to the boil. A small squeeze of lemon helps the mixture to jell. When the syrup is thick, remove the pan from the stove, allow to cool and put the jam into jars.

KABAK REÇELİ VE TATLISI

(PUMPKIN JAM AND PUMPKIN SWEET)

2 lbs pumpkins   ½ hour

1½ lbs sugar

¼ lb almonds

Slice the pumpkins and remove the skin and pips. Cut up the flesh into attractive shapes and boil them in water until tender. Drain, and stick a blanched almond into each piece. Boil them again, this time with sugar and a little water until the syrup thickens. Cool and put into jars. Walnuts can be used instead of almonds and sometimes the same recipe is done with slices of pumpkin instead of small shapes. Then ground walnuts can be sprinkled over them. This is served as a sweet course rather than jam.

AŞURE

(WHEAT PUDDING)

½ lb split wheat   3 hours

1 pint milk

2 ozs sultanas

A few pieces of orange peel

3 tablespoons sugar

2 ozs almonds

¼ lb sesami seeds

Soak the wheat overnight. Next day cook the wheat with plenty of water until tender (this may take anything up to 3 hours). Test the wheat to make sure it is soft, then add the milk, sultanas, orange peel and sugar. Cook slowly, until thick and creamy. Put into bowls, sprinkle with sesame seeds and decorate with a few almonds. Allow to set. (In fact, this is best eaten the following day).

This type of wheat is not easy to get in this country but the occasional oriental store has it. You can buy it in quantity and store it as it keeps perfectly.

KOLİFA

(BOILED KERNELS OF WHEAT)

3 hours

This is usually cooked to celebrate the first tooth of the

baby. It is something like Aşure but for Kolifa the wheat is cooked whole and served with sesame seeds, raisins, nuts and sugar.

MAHALLEBİ

(TURKISH BLANCMANGE)

10 minutes

This is a milk pudding like custard only it is thickened with ground rice instead of custard powder. It sets and is eaten cold.

1 pint milk

2 tablespoons ground rice

2 tablespoons sugar

Heat the milk and when it is warm dissolve the ground rice and sugar with a little of it. Pour this mixture into the saucepan when the rest of the milk is hot and cook slowly until it thickens. Pour into a bowl and let it set. Decorate with blanched almonds.

YOGURT (PLAIN)

½ pint milk   5 - 6 hours

2 teaspoons live yogurt (commercial yogurt will do)

Boil the milk and then let it cool to slightly above blood temperature, (test it by dipping your little finger in it: it must feel hot but not burn you). Take two tablespoons of milk out of this and mix the yogurt into a smooth cream with it in the carton. Pour the rest of the milk on top, cover with a lid and stand in a warm place (airing cupboard ideal if you have one) for 3 hours on a hot day, 5 hours on a cold day. By this time the yogurt will have set. Take the lid off and put it in the fridge, and use when required.

DRIED FRUIT

In Turkey, as well as in Cyprus, there is plenty of fresh fruit. Consequently, quite a lot is dried, especially apricots, figs and raisins.

Apart from just having stewed fruit, there is a way of cooking dried apricots which is worth mentioning:

1 cup sugar	1 cup dried apricots
2 ozs almonds	2 or 3 cups water

Boil the apricots first with the water. When nearly tender, add the sugar and almonds and boil together for a little while longer until the apricots are quite soft. Serve hot.

HELLİM

(SOFT CHEESE)

2 pints milk   3 teaspoons Rennet

Warm the milk to blood temperature, add the Rennet and let it set in a warm place. When set, break up the junket with your hands. Put the pan on a slow heat until all the whey comes up to the surface. Strain the whey into another pan and collect the bits of cheese, shaping them into a pattern. Boil up the whey and put the cheese you have shaped into it. When the cheese is cooked (it comes up to the surface), remove it from the whey, salt it and sprinkle with mint. Leave it to cool and try eating it when it is so fresh that it squeaks when you cut it.

It is absolutely delicious with sweet and water melon, grapes or fresh figs; equally delicious with cucumber or tomatoes.

When it is more mature, like the Hellim you can buy commercially, you can slice it, grill it on sesame bread or toast, or fry it with eggs for breakfast.

SİMİT HELVA

(SEMOLINA PUDDING)

½ hour

¼ lb butter	½ lb sugar
¼ lb almonds	5 cups water
½ lb semolina	

Melt the butter in a preserving pan or a thick saucepan. Add blanched almonds and when they turn pink in colour add semolina. Keep stirring with a wooden spoon. Make a thin syrup by boiling the sugar and the water. When semolina is cooked (i.e. when it does not stick to the sides of the pan any more), pour the hot syrup into it and stir.

Leave it for a few minutes and serve hot.

KARPUZ REÇELİ

(WATER MELON PRESERVE)

1 thick-skinned water melon	1 hour
2 tablespoons lime	
1½ cups sugar	
1 cup water	
Lemon juice	
½ teaspoon vanilla essence	

Cut a water melon into slices. Eat the edible part then cut the peel into 2 inch squares and peel off the green part on the outside. Wash these under the tap and put them into a bowl with cold water just covering them. Add the lime and leave to stand for 2 hours to harden the peel, stirring from time to time. Then wash it under a cold tap and boil in water for 20 minutes until the peel is soft. Remove from the pan and throw away the water. Make a syrup with the sugar and the water by boiling the two together. Add a few drops of lemon juice and vanilla essence and then the peel. Boil for another 20 minutes until the syrup thickens further. Then spread the peel on to a plate and, when slightly dry, sprinkle with sugar and ginger.

YOĞURT TATLISI

(YOGURT PUDDING)

3 eggs   40 minutes

1 cup sugar

1 cup yogurt

2 cups flour

1 teaspoon bicarbonate of soda

Juice of ½ lemon

2 cups sugar

1½ cups water

Break the eggs into a bowl. Add the sugar and beat for a while. Then add the yogurt and flour, stirring all the time. Lastly add the bicarbonate of soda and the lemon juice. Put into a greased tin and bake in a medium oven for 35 to 40 minutes. Now make a syrup with the sugar and the water by boiling them together. When the syrup is cold and the mixture is baked, pour the cold syrup over the hot cake mixture. Cut into squares and serve cold.

KADIN GÖBEĞİ

(WOMAN'S NAVEL)

1 lb shortcrust pastry   ½ hour

¼ lb walnuts (or almonds)

1 teaspoon powdered cinnamon

1 teaspoon sugar

Roll out the pastry thinly into one or more sheets about 15 inch square. Grind the nuts, mix with the teaspoon of sugar and cinnamon and sprinkle over the sheet of pastry. Cut the pastry into 3 inch wide strips and pleat each strip 3 or 4 times so that it becomes ¼ inch high and ¼ inch wide. Coil each strip clockwise to make a pastry (like a smaller edition of a Danish bun) about 2½ inch diameter. Place them on greased trays and bake for ½ an hour in a medium oven. While still hot drop them into cold syrup. Remove from syrup before serving.

GÜLLAÇ

(RICE PAPER SOAKED IN SYRUP)

10 minutes

¼ lb almonds	Rosewater
2 tablespoons sugar	2 cups sugar
1 tablespoon cinnamon	1 cup water

Güllaç

Prepare the filling first by blanching the almonds and chopping them into small pieces. Add the sugar and cinnamon and mix well. Allow one sheet of güllaç per person.

(It looks like rice paper.) Wet it with water and a few drops of rosewater. Fold it into a square, put the filling in, roll like a sausage and place on a pyrex dish. Make a syrup with the water and the sugar by boiling them together for 5 minutes. Pour the syrup over the güllaç and wait for it to be absorbed. Serve cold.

LOKMA

(DOUGHNUTS)

3 tablespoons flour   ½ hour

1 oz fresh yeast

1 cup warm water

Oil for frying

Sieve the flour and rub the yeast into this as if you were rubbing butter. Make a hole in the centre and slowly add the warm water, stirring all the time with a wooden spoon, until it is the consistency of thick batter. Leave it to stand for 5 minutes. Make a syrup by boiling 2 cups of sugar and one cup of water. Let it cool and pour into a large bowl.

Fill a large frying pan with cooking oil and heat well. Drop teaspoonfuls of batter into the hot fat. They will rise quickly in the shape of little balls and when they are pink, drop them into cold syrup which they will absorb almost immediately. Put on another dish and serve hot or cold.

MAKRUN

(MACAROONS)

½ lb walnuts   20 minutes

1 tablespoon cinnamon

2 tablespoons sugar

1 lb semolina

1 teaspoon baking powder

¼ lb unsalted butter or Spry

1 cup water

Grind the nuts and mix with the cinnamon and sugar. Put the semolina into a basin, add the baking powder and the melted butter, and mix. Add the water slowly and make a soft dough. Take a piece of dough in your hand and shape it into a round 'nut' with a hole in the middle. Fill the hole with the mixture of ground walnuts, cinnamon and sugar. Close the hole leaving a point, put on to greased trays and bake for 20 minutes, but do not let them get brown. When cooked, drop into cold syrup. The syrup is the same consistency as for Kadın Göbeği.

For variety, substitute chopped dates for walnuts.

BURMA KADEYİF

(PASTRY IN SYRUP)

¼ lb walnuts   ¾ hour

1 tablespoon sugar

1 teaspoon cinnamon

1 lb ready-made Paklava pastry

syrup of ½ lb of sugar

2 ozs unsalted butter

Grind the nuts and mix with the sugar and cinnamon. Separate the layers of pastry and sprinkle on each a few drops of melted butter and the mixture of ground nuts, sugar and cinnamon. Roll round a rolling pin (the rolling pin used for this purpose is long and thin rather than short and dumpy. A wooden dowell rod makes a satisfactory Turkish rolling pin). Pull away the rolling pin and as it is withdrawn, the pastry will fall into a concertina shape, forming a wrinkled tube. Put on a greased tray and bake in a medium oven for about three-quarters of an hour. When they are nicely pink pour cold syrup over them and let the pastry absorb the syrup while still in the tray. Later cut into portions and serve.

SWEET WINES

It is strange that you do not see sweet white table wines very often in Turkey. This is possibly how the tradition of serving sweets to guests with a cup of Turkish coffee instead of wine, came about, for the syrup with which most sweets are soaked demands a wine as sweet as a Barsac or an Haut Sauternes.

In Cyprus you can have Commandaria, still made from the original vineyards of the Commandery of St. John of Jerusalem, dating back to the Crusades or earlier. Indeed, the Talmud names Cyprus wines as the first choice among sweet wines.

Commandaria made from red grapes is more like a Port, but the rare White Commandaria is a little bit like the Vins Doux Naturels of the South of France, Frontignan and Roussillon.

Port and nuts traditionally go well together, so you can serve Port with such sweets as Baklava or Kadeyif.

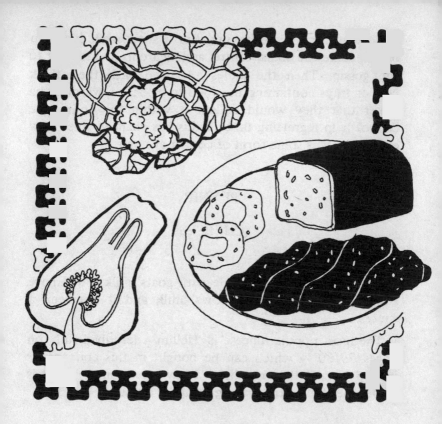

Bread, Cheese and Pickles

In the days when people did not have the luxury of ovens at home, anything that needed cooking had to go to the nearest baker. These bakers had old-fashioned ovens which were heated by wood and swept clean of the ashes. The dough was shaped by hand and the loaves were then put on a long wooden shovel and baked on the stone floor of the oven, so that when all the baking was done, one could see row upon row of lovely crisp, round loaves — never tin-shaped. The baker then used the hot oven to carry out his orders for private baking. For a short while his shop had become the social centre, adding aroma and flavour to the gossip. Then the ladies advanced with their thick copper trays containing the food to be baked, warning the baker that they would collect it within the hour. One cannot help regretting that all this has changed since now everyone owns some form of cooker at home.

PEYNİR

(CHEESES)

Locally cheeses are all made with goats' milk. But I have tried making them with cows' milk and it has been a success.

The most popular cheese is 'Hellim'– described fully on pages 79/80 – which can be bought in this country, as indeed can all the ingredients I have mentioned. But it is sometimes fun to try making things at home.

SİMİT or ÇÖREK

(SESAME BREAD)

1 lb flour	1 oz fresh yeast
1 teaspoon salt	sesame seeds

Sieve the flour with the salt into a basin. Cream the yeast with a little warm water and add to the flour. Add a little more warm water, making a soft dough. Knead well and leave for half an hour in a warm place. When the dough has risen, knead once more and shape into a roll of 8 to 10 inches long. Mark with the back of a knife six times. Brush the top with a little milk and sprinkle thickly with sesame seeds. Bake in a medium oven for half an hour or until pink.

DARI UNU İLE YAPILMIŞ EKMEK

(CORN BREAD)

1 cup maize flour	40 minutes

3 tablespoons sugar

3 teaspoons baking powder

1 teaspoon salt

1 cup corn meal

1 egg

1½ cups milk

¼ cup oil

If you can't get maize flour, use wheat flour

Sift dry ingredients into a basin. Combine egg, milk and oil and add to the dry ingredients. Mix until smooth. Put into a greased tin and bake in a medium to low oven for about 40 minutes.

NOR

(WHEY CHEESE)

1 pint milk	10 - 15 minutes

1 teaspoon vinegar (optional)

This is a cream cheese, made to use up the whey left over from making Hellim. To the whey add the milk and stand the pan on a low heat. The milk will curdle but if it takes too long to curdle, add the vinegar. Strain through a fine sieve and place on a dish. Serve with sugar or salt.

TURŞU

(PICKLES)

Pickles are an essential part of a Turkish housewife's larder. As each meal requires a green salad it is only natural to provide an alternative. The most common pickle is a mixed vegetable including fresh celery, cucumber, and green peppers.

Chop these up into 2-inch pieces, wash well and leave in salty water for 24 hours. Remove the vegetables, wash and leave to drain for a few hours. Then put them into a jar and cover with malt vinegar.

ZEYTİN BİTTASI

(OLIVE BREAD)

2 eggs   ½ hour

½ cup milk

½ cup water

1½ cups flour

1 teaspoon baking powder

1 teaspoon salt

4 tablespoons olive oil

1 cup black olives

1 teaspoon mint

Beat the eggs in a large basin. Add the milk and water. Sieve the flour with the baking powder and the salt and add gradually to the liquid. Add the cooking oil and the olives from which the stones have been removed, then the mint, and mix it all together. It should have the consistency of a cake mixture. Grease a (tea-)cake tray, put the mixture in it and bake for half an hour in a medium oven.

LAHANA TURŞUSU

(CAULIFLOWER PICKLE)

Dough   Mustard powder

Cauliflower   Salt

One loaf of uncooked bread (if you can induce your baker to let you have it) would cut the work involved by half. This dough is then kept for 8 days until it ferments.

Cut the cauliflower into flowerets and remove all the green leaves. Wash the flowerets and put them into boiling water, boil once for a few minutes. Take them out and now remove the hard crust of the dough. Melt the remaining dough with a little warm water and dip each spring of cauliflower into it. Then sprinkle each floweret liberally with mustard powder and salt and put into a jar. Pour the remaining dough over it, put on the lid of the jar and leave for 3 days. Shake the jar of pickles once a day as the dough usually gathers at the bottom. It can be eaten about the 5th day.

This is one of the more difficult pickles but it is well worth the effort.

DRINK WITH CHEESE

In England, bread and cheese and pickles are traditionally accompanied by a mug of beer or ale, or a pitcher of hard cider: all the better if it is home-brewed.

Although there are good breweries in Turkey and Cyprus, there is no tradition of home-brewed beer. Maybe this is because there is no surplus of cereals.

On the other hand, the olives and the grapes grow freely, and the residues (the olive-stones and the pips and the skins of the grapes) are fermented and home-distilled to provide a potent local fire-water called Zivania. The French equivalent of this is 'Marc', which means 'murky'.

Turkish Coffee

Turkish coffee follows every meal in Turkish homes; without it the meal is not complete. It is so simple to make and yet even among Turkish ladies there are those who can and those who cannot make perfect coffee. It's just a knack: the art lies in whether you can produce a thick foam on top of each cup.

Turkish coffee is part of the social system. It's the remedy for everything. It's the cure for headaches. It's the accompaniment to trik-trak (that Turkish substitute for the game of draughts in the coffee shop).

It was the food of kings and sultans. There is a good story about Abdul Hamid II who built various kiosks all over the palace garden and each one was decorated just like a coffee-shop. They were kept open at night for Abdul Hamid would suddenly walk in, order a coffee and pay for it. The coffee certainly had to be good.

This is the recipe:

Choose a brand of coffee you like and have it ground. Ask for it to be pulverised. You must have a coffee pot which you can heat over a flame. Usually it is made of copper but aluminium will do. For each cup you allow one level teaspoon of sugar and one heaped teaspoon of coffee. Put them both into the warm water and stir until the sugar is dissolved. Put over a low heat and bring to the boil. It must not boil over, but only come up to a rising boil.

Now the ceremony of pouring out the coffee starts: the coffee cups must be as elegant as possible. The coffee pot is gently tapped on the side of the stove; this allows the coffee grains to fall to the bottom. A little of the coffee is poured into each cup, so that each has some of the foam or 'cream' of the coffee. Then the cups are filled and offered round. It is then sipped slowly − each mouthful to be savoured and enjoyed . . . .

COFFEE AND LIQUEURS

In Turkey, brandy is drunk before the meal as a long drink, and not normally (as with French Cognac) sipped from a balloon glass with the coffee. Yet distilling is not a mystery in Turkey or Cyprus − many a household has its still.

When the roses are blooming in the gardens, the petals are gathered, and distilled into rosewater or essence of roses. So it is natural that Turkey should produce a sweet Rose Liqueur − Gül Likör. One Turkish mint liqueur which I tasted − Nane Likör − differed from Crème de Menthe in that it did not have the overpowering peppermint taste of most French mint liqueurs; it was a subtle blend of peppermint, spearmint and garden mint.

To match its finesse in a liqueur available in the West, you must try Royal Mint - Chocolate Liqueur, a new introduction with the ever-popular flavour of after-dinner mints.

In Turkey the most popular liqueurs are Strawberry (Vişne Likör) and Cherry (Kiraz Likör).

A speciality known and appreciated outside Turkey is Mersin, a fine liqueur — not too sweet — made from highly aromatic Myrtleberries.

STORE CUPBOARD

The pictures on the left show typical Turkish kitchen implements and a few ingredients such as Tahini, a creamy sesame seed paste which is the foundation of several dips. You can also see a cezve (pronounced jezveh) or coffee-saucepan, a coarse sieve, tea glasses and saucers, a pestle and mortar, and various other things.

To help those who have difficulty in obtaining ingredients, I list three London firms who between them stock everything and who will deal by post.

The Greek Food Centre.
12 Inverness Street,
London, N.W.1.
01-485-6544

The Istanbul Emporium.
477-479, Liverpool Road,
London, N.7.
01-607-2045

 and at

58, Cross Street,
London, N.1.
01-226-9168

PSP Continental Pastries Ltd.
9, Kentish Town Road,
Kentish Town,
London, N.W.1.
01-GUL-7518

A Spicy Dish

Simple mixtures of the freshest of ingredients, served together or cooked slowly together to achieve a mingling of flavours — this is the basis of Turkish cooking. Neighbouring countries influenced by the Turkish culture, have borrowed recipes and produced local variations. As a generalisation, you might say that Greek cooking is oilier, Arabic cooking spicier, while Persian cooking (and perhaps the Parsee dishes of India) turns the Turkish Pilaf into something approaching a mild curry.

I have therefore given you the recipes in their simplest form, and you can, if you wish, try out the spicier and more exotic variations by adding some of the following spices:

MINT   (Nane) can be mixed with cheese sprinkled over macaroni; fresh mint can be added to a salad of cos lettuce dressed with vinegar in preference to lemon-juice; it can be made into refreshing and digestive mint tea; and it is an essential ingredient of cacik (see Hors d'Oeuvres chapter).

PAPRIKA (Biber) is a mild red pepper used to decorate humus.

GARLIC (Sarmısak) is a matter for discretion or social conscience; large-scale use gives the effect of Armenian cooking.

99

CLOVES (Karanfil) are not so much used in Turkish cookery, but may be used to neutralise the smell of garlic on the breath. Is it not strange that we speak of a clove of garlic?

CINNAMON (Tarçın) is used in many interesting ways — it can be sprinkled very discreetly into pilaff to enrich the flavour, and it is used with nuts in the fillings of sweet pastries like Paklava and Kadin Gobegi.

ROSEWATER (Gülsuyu) can be used to flavour syrup poured over sweet pastries, and can perfume the Turkish version of Blancmange — Mahallebi (Chapter 7)

MASTIK (Sakız) is sometimes used to flavour sweets (in Cyprus it is used in Turkish delight). It is a gum, and oddly enough, you can chew it!

PINE NUTS (Sunu Biber) impart a faintly resinous, nutty taste to pilaff.

CARAWAY (Keraviye)

SAGE (Adaçayı)

PARSLEY (Maidanoz) is chopped up to flavour kofte and dolma, mixed with tomato and raw onion to serve with kebab, and used to garnish many dishes, such as humus.

CORIANDER (Kolyandro) can be bought as seeds, and ground as a spice. In Cyprus, however, the seeds are sown in the garden, and the long straggly plants are added to salads, to give a most unusual flavour. It grows easily in this country.

CUMIN (Kimyon) seed is a relative of caraway, but more strongly flavoured. It is used powdered, to add interest to meat stews, giving a dish something like a very mild, but spicy brown curry flavour.

THYME (Kekik) is also used to flavour meat dishes.

SUMACH (Sumak). The coarsely ground seeds give a reddish-brown spice with a light - almost lemon sorrel - flavour. It can be used as a garnish for humus, and as an important ingredient for sumakli köfte.

ELDERFLOWERS (Murver) are dried and used to make a refreshing tea.

SAFFRON (Safran) can be added to a pilaff, making it taste like a Persian pilau. Or a dolma can be made, wrapped in a cabbage leaf, and spiced with saffron, which is an Arabic version of a Turkish recipe.

TURKISH INDEX

ENGLISH INDEX

Inscription on cover: An ancient Turkish prayer
'In the name of God I set forth'—*Calligrapher unknown*

First published 1968 by
Tredolphin Press, London
Published as a Paperback 1970
© Nezih Simon

SBN 900288 01 9

Illustrations by Jean Papworth
Artwork and layout by Jill Vasey
Cover design by Peter Ballard

Printed Offset Litho and bound in Great Britain by
Cox & Wyman Ltd, London, Fakenham and Reading